SCOTLAND IN OLD HS

AROUND LOCHABER

FIONA MACLEAN

SUTTON PUBLISHING LIMITED

Sutton Publishing Limited
Phoenix Mill · Thrupp · Stroud
Gloucestershire · GL5 2BU

First published 1996

Copyright © Fiona Maclean, 1996

Cover photographs: *front:* The first motorized
ascent of Ben Nevis, 1911; *back:* Maclean of
Ardgour on the hill, 1920s.

British Library Cataloguing in Publication Data
A catalogue record for this book is available from the
British Library.

ISBN 0-7509-1265-0

Typeset in 10/12 Perpetua.
Typesetting and origination by
Sutton Publishing Limited.
Printed in Great Britain by
Ebenezer Baylis, Worcester.

CONTENTS

Inverlochy Castle, *c.* 1900. Inverlochy was the original heart of the Lordship of Lochaber. This great castle was built in about 1280 by the Comyn Lords of Lochaber, Guardians of the Realm with, among others, John Balliol and Robert the Bruce. It reflects a time when Lochaber was less isolated from national politics.

Kinlochaline Castle before its 'restoration' by the Smiths of Ardtornish Estate in the 1890s. A typical fifteenth-century tower house, it fell into disuse after 1679, when the Campbells seized it from the Macleans.

INTRODUCTION

What is Lochaber? Lochaber's boundaries have fluctuated greatly through history, but the name itself is probably derived from the marshy loch that would have covered the moss between Fort William and Corpach.

The Lordship of Lochaber stretched from the River Spey to the Atlantic when Macbeth disposed of its Thane, Banquo. The MacDonald Lords of the Isles became Lords of Lochaber from the fourteenth century and under their rule the clan system flourished. The Lordship of the Isles was dissolved in 1493 and King James IV granted the Lordship of Lochaber to Alexander Gordon, 3rd Earl of Huntly, in 1505. This grant gave the Earl legal jurisdiction over a large area of the west coast, but in reality the Lochaber clans held their lands by force of arms. The MacDonells of Keppoch had, for instance, forfeited their lands as followers of the Lord of the Isles, but the Earl could not dislodge them. The Camerons and the Mackintoshes were to dispute ownership of Glen Loy and Loch Arkaig for over 350 years until 1665. At that time 'Lochaber Men' simply denoted the races of cattle dealers, and on occasion cattle rustlers, that lived beyond the Moor of Rannoch.

For the purposes of this book Lochaber generally follows the mainland boundaries of the present-day district, from Mallaig down to Ballachulish, and as far east as Invergarry.[1]

Lochaber is a very beautiful area, with its high mountains and deep glens. It was very isolated until the last century. With its heavy rainfall and lack of good farmland, its people were forced to live as subsistence farmers. Its population remained thinly scattered and its social structure – based on the clan system – remained virtually unchanged for centuries.

The area had been detached from national politics for a time when in 1645 the Royalist Marquis of Montrose won a sweeping victory over the Marquis of Argyll at Inverlochy. Nine years later General Monk, to establish a stronghold in Lochaber for the Cromwellian Government, built a wood and turf fort where the River Nevis entered Loch Linnhe. From 1688, and the accession of William and Mary, Lochaber was to be at

---

[1] Knoydart has not been included. An extensive collection of photographs of the peninsula can be seen at the Mallaig Heritage Centre.

the heart of the Jacobite movement. After the Lochaber chiefs had risen with Claverhouse in 1689, General Mackay rebuilt the fort in stone. Somewhat defiantly, he named the fortress Fort William and the cluster of huts below the fort walls Maryburgh. General Wade, in his mission to pacify the Highlands after the 1715 Rising, strengthened the fort further, and built a road to connect it with Fort Augustus. The siting of the fort was amply justified when Prince Charles Edward Stuart landed at Moidart in 1745, and raised his standard to rally the clans at Glenfinnan.

The defeat of the Jacobite cause at Culloden in 1746 was to effect great social upheaval throughout the Highlands, and nowhere more than in Lochaber. The Hanoverian Government was determined to break the clan system, and indeed the harryings and forfeiture of land in Lochaber after Culloden was an effective start to this policy. The Government removed any remaining 'right of heritable jurisdiction' from the clan chiefs, and from this point the chiefs were to become increasingly distanced from their clansmen. Lands traditionally held on behalf of the clan were to be sold to wealthy incomers. Highlanders had always seen land as a communal resource; now it became a resource to be exploited for individual profit. Landowners established crofting communities, moving their people out of the glens to make way for the sheep. The first of the lowland graziers arrived, and land that had been farmed by a community on the 'run-rig' system now became open grazings. By the turn of the century, emigration, often of whole communities led by their tacksman or senior tenant, had begun and was to continue throughout the nineteenth century.

The first emigrant ship left Maryburgh in 1773. The growing township, which in time took on the name Fort William, was to become one of the seven main points of departure for emigrants; in 1801 alone, eleven ships sailed from the town carrying 3,300 emigrants. There were many direct reasons for the emigrations of the nineteenth century – the collapse in the price of kelp ash in the 1820s, or the failure of the potato crop in 1846 were examples of this – but basically the land available in the Highlands was too poor to support its existing population.

At the beginning of the nineteenth century the Government in London commissioned Thomas Telford, the great engineer, to report on ways in which the flood of emigration and general economic deprivation in the Highlands could be relieved. His proposals were to affect Lochaber in three ways. Firstly, Telford designed and oversaw the building of the Caledonian Canal from Inverness to Fort William until its completion in 1822. Secondly, he organised the building of new roads; his first commission in Lochaber was the building of a road from Fort William to Arisaig in 1803, to be followed by Corran to Kinlochmoidart, Glengarry through to the head of Loch Hourn, and Spean Bridge to Kingussie. Thirdly, the same Parliamentary Commissioners for whom Telford worked engaged him to design a simple church and manse for a series of new parishes in the Highlands; Lochaber was to have four of these 'Parliamentary' churches. Lochaber, together with the rest of the

Highlands, was being opened up by serious Government investment. Towards the end of the century, agitation among the crofting community about their conditions of tenure led to the Government setting up the Napier Commission. This Commission published its report in 1883 and among its many proposals made clear that the Highlands needed improved communications. Discussion was revived about building a West Highland railway, and in 1894 the West Highland Railway Company finally linked Glasgow with Fort William. The greatest step in breaking down Lochaber's isolation had been achieved. The railway was extended to Mallaig, and its herring fleets, in 1901.

This century has seen the development of large-scale industry in Lochaber. The area's high rainfall and steep mountains made it very suitable for the development of hydro-electric schemes. This led to the British Aluminium Company establishing smelters at Kinlochleven and Fort William. In the 1960s, as part of the Wilson Government's policy of decentralisation, Wiggins Teape built a pulp and paper mill at Corpach. By 1966, 45 per cent of Lochaber's population was living in the Fort William area.

Today the population of Lochaber is increasing, but notably more in the country areas. The establishment of salmon farms has brought employment to existing rural communities. A granite superquarry at remote Glensanda on Loch Linnhe transports workers in by sea. Tourism continues to expand, and the development of a ski area in the shadow of Ben Nevis is set to extend the area's tourist season. Lochaber's economy has come a long way from the days of one based on cattle-dealing; the current emphasis on keeping alive the Gaelic language and therefore its culture is a sign of the area's new confidence. The last hundred years have seen immense changes in Lochaber, and this book reflects some of these changes.

Invergarry Castle and Loch Lochy, *c.* 1900. The present castle, built by the MacDonells of Glengarry, dates from the end of the seventeenth century. It was burnt after Culloden and the Chiefs of Glengarry had sold all their lands but the castle by 1860.

THE BURGH

Colin Young, first Provost of Fort William, 1892. It was during his term of office that the railway came to Fort William. Provost Young was also Master of the Fort William Masonic Lodge in 1892. There was a Lodge in Fort William by 1736.

The burgh of Fort William began as a cluster of sutlers' huts below the walls of the Fort. This township was called Maryburgh by General Mackay when he rebuilt and renamed Fort William in 1690, and it was subsequently confirmed as a 'burgh of barony'.

The settlement was establishing itself as a trading centre independent of the fort and with its own customs post when it was destroyed in 1746. The fort was preparing for the Jacobite siege, and the buildings were cleared as they restricted its line of fire. The township was quickly re-established, and by the beginning of the nineteenth century it stretched out along the line of the military road to the south. Two parallel streets ran between this High Street and the lochside. By 1875, when nine Commissioners were elected by the male householders of the town to oversee water and policing, the burgh was generally known as Fort William. The first Burgh Council was elected in 1892.

The arrival of the West Highland Railway in 1894 had a tremendous effect on the economy of the whole area. With the increased tourist traffic, public buildings and bridges were constructed and improved and the burgh of Fort William prospered.

Children playing below West End pier, Fort William, 1920s. This pier predates the pier at Station Square. The beach has now been filled in and is covered by the bypass.

T R A N S P O R T

The Fort from Cow Hill, before 1890. Built at the confluence of the River Nevis and Loch Linnhe, the fort on its triangular site is cut off from the mainland by a deep ditch. The site was a good one; during the Jacobite siege of Fort William in 1746, Government ships were able to keep contact with the garrison of over 600 men virtually unopposed. The River Nevis was diverted in the early 1970s.

The fort from the land side, before 1890. The last regular garrison left in 1854, the houses of the fort became private accommodation, and the moat became a vegetable patch. From 1889 much of the fort was demolished by the West Highland Railway Company to build engine sheds.

Ceremony of dedication of the Arch at the entrance to The Craigs Burial Ground, 1896. The inner arch of the fort was moved to the spot where the first Cameron Highlanders, raised in 1793 by Sir Alan Cameron of Erracht, were sworn in.

Fort William before the railway. St Andrew's Episcopal church was built in 1880. The architect for this attractive building was Dr Alexander Ross of Inverness, who also built the Choir School on the far left. The old rectory on the left of the church was demolished in 1958.

Fort William, early 1900s. The railway now runs along the foreshore. A corner of Duncansburgh church is on the left, and Tweeddale Gardens, which served as a hostel for railway workers, is in front of St Andrew's church.

Building the West Highland Railway, Loch Treig, 1890s. Crossing the Moor of Rannoch had been a technical challenge as the railway had to float on the bog. This stage of the construction was much easier as a boat could be used for supplies.

Steam navvy at Auchnadaull, near Fort William, 1890s. The railway was built as cheaply as possible as it was assumed that traffic would be comparatively light.

Fort William pier, east. The pier was built specifically for railway supplies. The fort houses are still intact. This pier was further west than the present pier.

Breaching the fort walls, 1889. The fort's proprietor had stipulated in his will that the ground should be used by the railway, should the latter reach the town. The railway achieved what the Jacobites had failed to do in 1746.

The first train arrives at Fort William on completion of the West Highland line, 1894. The opening ceremony was performed by Lady Abinger of Inverlochy Castle, whose husband was the first chairman of the West Highland Railway Company.

Fort William station soon after completion. It was a controversial decision at the time to take the railway along the foreshore to the steamer pier, and it led to the town being cut off from its lochside shoreline.

Steamer at Corpach, 1890s. Steamers plied daily from Glasgow, and passengers transferred by coach to canal steamers. The building on the right was the original pump house, demolished in 1968, and that on the left is now the British Waterway Board's office.

SS *Gondolier* leaving Banavie. The branch line to the top of the first flight of locks was built in 1895 and passengers walked up from the terminus below the canal. This goods engine has shunted up a 1 in 24 incline. The *Gondolier* plied between Fort William and Inverness for over seventy years from 1866. She was to be sunk at Scapa Flow in 1939.

Neptune's Staircase, Banavie, 1920s. This first flight of eight locks climbs 72 ft. In the 1840s the canal was extended and deepened, but it is essentially little changed from that which Telford designed a hundred years before.

Damage to lock gates on Neptune's Staircase, 1929. A herring drifter rammed two lock gates, luckily with no loss of life, and the canal was closed for three months. The building on the right is one of the two bow-fronted foremen's houses at Banavie designed by Telford.

HMS *Brierton* coming through the locks at Banavie, 1965. This must have been one of the last times that the capstans were used before, to the relief of canal users, they were replaced by the present hydraulic system.

Banavie Hotel after fire, 1924. Built in 1848, the hotel was a vital staging post for passengers transferring from canal steamers. It was a military hospital during the First World War. Stones from the building were used in the new Lochy Bridge.

The Victoria suspension bridge over the Lochy before it was replaced in 1929. This graceful bridge was built in 1848 by Donald Cameron, 23rd of Lochiel. The toll house on the west side charged the equivalent of the former ferry fare.

Lochy Bridge looking west, 1930s. The arches are those of the original suspension bridge. The bridge was eventually replaced in the 1960s; traffic by then was somewhat heavier than in this photograph.

Angus Cameron, auctioneer, 1892. Mr Cameron established the first regular Mart in 1888 at Lochybridge, before moving to Nevis Bridge. His grandson owns Glen Nevis farm, and a great-grandson runs Peter MacLennan's shop in the High Street.

Old Nevis Bridge, 1909. The arch is for King Edward VII, coming to stalk at Mamore. Queen Victoria had driven straight through an earlier celebration arch at Roy Bridge, and regretted subsequently that she had failed to stop.

BEN NEVIS

Looking across the north face of Ben Nevis to the observatory and hotel, early 1900s. The Ben, at 4,418 ft, is literally at the heart of Lochaber's tourist industry. The observatory and wooden hotel were built in 1883. The observatory was abandoned in 1904, and the hotel, which offered meals and could sleep up to twelve guests, closed in 1915.

Track up to the summit, 1883. The path, which begins at Achintee Farm, was paid for by public subscription in order to build the observatory. Pack ponies were used to bring up building supplies.

Building the observatory, 1883. The observatory was constructed, again by public subscription, specifically to observe a period of sunspot activity. The round wooden tower held recording instruments, but it also provided an emergency exit if the observatory was snowed under.

Inside the observatory. A daily record of the weather was telegraphed and subsequently telephoned to Fort William. The man seated may be William Kilgour, one of the first modern historians of Lochaber.

Climbing the Ben, early 1900s. It would be hard to imagine anyone climbing so cheerfully today in these clothes.

First Ben Nevis Hill Race, 1903. William Swan, third from left, a Fort William tobacconist, was in 1895 the first man to record how long he took to climb the Ben. This race was from Achintee Farm, and six out of the seven men were local. The winner was Ewen MacKenzie, possibly the second runner on the right. Ewen was the observatory roadman, so he could be said to have a natural advantage. His time, set later in the year, was not beaten until 1938. The Ben Race in 1985 had 500 entrants.

The first motorised ascent of the Ben, 1911. Henry Alexander from Edinburgh took five days to drive –
and push – his Model T Ford up the observatory road to the summit.

Henry Alexander at the summit. Henry's father had the main agency for Ford cars in Edinburgh, so it is
probable that he had mixed motives for making this tremendous ascent.

THE TOWN

High Street looking east, 1890s. This elegant street depicts a different town to that described fifty years
before as dirty and with 'dram houses without number'. Behind this street, however, the buildings were
less salubrious. In 1895 the Masons threatened to evict their ground-floor tenant unless he removed his
cow and other livestock from behind their High Street building. MacFarlanes the chemist on the right is
one of the oldest shops in the town, and has been in operation since 1852.

High Street looking east, *c.* 1900. The Free Church is in the distance, and the new building on the left is now The Drovers bar. The photographer would today be standing in the middle of the road opposite the police station.

Tailors at MacKinnon's, High Street, 1890s. A glimpse of the labour that went into tailoring. Duncan MacKinnon himself, possibly the man in the foreground, was a much-valued Burgh Councillor.

Electricity hut at Blarmachfoldach. Fort William was, in 1896, the first town in Britain to have hydro-powered electric street lighting. A dam on the River Kiachnish provided the source of power.

Police station, Fort William, *c.* 1900. The building had also served as the town's courthouse and jail until the present courthouse was built in 1879. This fine building was replaced by the present police station in 1971.

Fort William School, early 1900s. The school was built after the Education Act of 1872, which made education compulsory and was to see the end of Gaelic as the first language of the Highlands. The previous high school had been where the West End Hotel now stands; its standard had declined during the period of emigrations. This building was to serve until the new high school was built in 1960, whereupon the primary school next door took it on. The little boy in the kilt does not appear to be enjoying his audience.

Return of the Lovat Scouts and Cameron Volunteers from the Boer War, 1901. Lord Lovat had seen the need for a regiment of men with hillcraft and shooting skills to match those of the Boers. His Lovat Scouts were a hand-picked group of stalkers and ghillies from the Highlands, and they proved invaluable in South Africa. The homecoming of these first Scouts would have been an emotional one.

Parade of Lovat Scouts and Cameron Volunteers in front of the Town Hall, Cameron Square. The Scouts retained their Highland identity; Lt. Col. A. William Macdonald of Blarour DSO commanded a regiment in the First World War, and Lt. Col. Donald Cameron of Lochiel, ygr, commanded the Scouts for the last year of the Second World War.

The Kennedy Memorial, Cameron Square, before 1907. The memorial was erected in 1852 to commemorate Dr William Kennedy who died of typhus contracted from the poor among whom he worked. The memorial was removed in 1965, and the stones dumped into Loch Linnhe.

Town Hall, Cameron Square. The original building (see above) was the Maryburgh church, built in 1790 and one of the oldest buildings in the town. It became the Town Hall, and was altered in 1907. The Town Hall was – memorably – burnt down in 1975.

NA H-UILE LATHA SONA DHUIBH

Greeting for Donald Cameron, 25th of Lochiel, and Lady Hermione, 1906. This arch at the Courthouse says 'May every day be happy for you'. The couple are returning from their wedding; the Burgh Council provides an imposing welcoming committee.

Belford Hospital, demolished in the 1960s. The building was on the site of the present Invernevis House and had some of the stones from the fort in its construction. The hospital was donated to the town in 1864 in the will of Andrew Belford of Glenfintaig, a notorious miser in his lifetime.

The fire engine of Fort William Distillery, 1890s. The 'Long John' Distillery had been established in 1825 by John Macdonald as the first 'legitimate still house' in Lochaber. This team of men contains two future Provosts of Fort William, Donald Shaw and Donald Cameron.

Blacksmith in Middle Street. This street is today a fast through road for motor traffic.

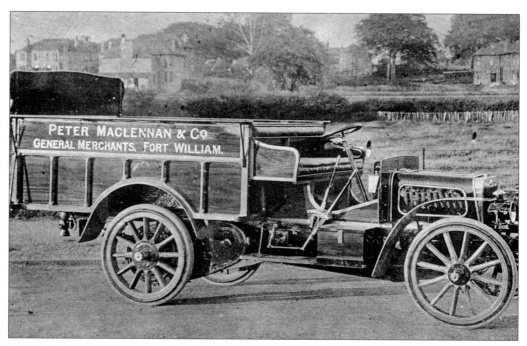

Peter MacLennan's van, *c.* 1910. This company is now the oldest in the High Street to be run by its founding family.

Marshall and Pearson's, with Colin Thomson, Davie Bryce and Dickie Cameron outside. It is still an ironmonger's today, but the goods for sale are rather different.

High Street looking east, with four very smart uniformed postmen. Queen Anne House is little changed today.

Mr Rodger and his daughter Bessie outside their tea-room. This building is just visible beyond Queen Anne House above. It has been replaced by a very modern building.

Diamond cutters at the Highland Hotel, 1919. After the First World War a workshop for disabled ex-servicemen, sponsored by the Oppenheimers, was set up in the hotel. The workshop was providing a training for men who might otherwise have been destitute.

Diamond cutters' outing to Roy Bridge, c. 1920; a contrast to what these men had been through in the trenches. The workshop was only short-lived.

Kenny Cameron's milk round, with Annie Chisholm in Lundavra Road.

Early traffic accident in Fort William, 1920s. The boy's reaction is timeless.

Disembarking at Fort William pier, *c.* 1910. The early history of the town revolved around the steamers; the Glasgow and Fort William Steamboat Company was founded in 1824. The last steamship to use the pier regularly was the TS *King George V*, who ended her weekly Fort William run in 1974.

Station Square looking towards the pier, 1920s. The fine street lamp on the right doubled as a horse trough.

Charabancs at Gordon Square, 1930s. Charabancs would meet the steamers and follow scheduled routes. This charabanc appears to have been hired for an outing. The building behind, now Macleod's, was the Station Hotel.

Station Square from steamer, 1930s. The station is on the left, Macrae and Dick's Garage — formerly St Mary's church and presbytery — at the top of the hill, and the Macbrayne's office on the right. The Highland Hotel behind was to be naval headquarters for the area during the Second World War.

Train pulling out of Fort William station, 1950s. The view from the station out over Loch Linnhe was unique. The station building was demolished in the early 1970s when the town's bypass was built along the lochside.

Railway sidings, 1960s. The sidings and old engine sheds were swept away when the railway station was moved to its present site in the early 1970s. Part of the fort walls are visible in the foreground.

Lochaber Home Guard on parade in George V Park, early 1940s. The Lochaber Defence Volunteers became the Home Guard in 1940. Their training ground was The Plantation, the area behind the town on the lower slopes of Cow Hill where there was a substantial stand of trees. Captain Harrold stands at the head of the Home Guard, with behind him, left to right, Sgts Steve Duthie, Lachie MacIntyre and Willie Foster.

Summer Training Camp at Scarborough, Lochaber Territorial Company, Queen's Own Cameron Highlanders, 1954. Among those present are: Back row, left to right: Ptes. Alan MacPherson, Coutts, Sinclair, Arthur Campbell, William Corrigan, William Kearney, Bernard Kearney, John MacGillivray, D.J. MacDonald, Murdo MacLeod, Dempster. Third row: Ptes. Craig, Goodwin, -?-, Archie MacDonald, -?-, Miller, Beaton, Nathaniel Rodgers, A.V. MacKenzie, Sinclair, Keenan. Second row: Cpl. MacKay, Cpl. Malcolm MacRaild, Ptes. Ronald Gillies, -?-, M. Cameron, MacMillan, Kenneth MacLeod, -?-, MacDonald, Robert Cameron, Peter MacDonald, Cpl. Neil MacVarish. Front row: Piper Alexander MacLeod, Lt. Blades, Sgt. MacPherson, Col. Donald Cameron of Lochiel, Sgt. Major Thomson, Lt. MacGregor, Sgt. Major Sinclair, Lt. MacKenzie, Sgt. Shearer, -?-, Cpl. Murray.

R E C R E A T I O N

Fort William Town Park, early 1900. The ground was given to the town in 1887 in commemoration of Queen Victoria's Jubilee. In 1936 it was renovated and its name changed from Jubilee Park to King George V Park. In 1969 the swimming pool was built on part of the land.

Lochaber Gathering, 1903. The Gathering was held at the Park until 1954. The old Belford Hospital is in the background, and the recently built Glenlochy Distillery on the right.

Gathering in Jubilee Park, mid-1920s. Donald Cameron of Lochiel, ygr, is on the right talking to Lt. Col. Alexander Maclean, 16th of Ardgour.

Alexander Anthony Cameron throwing the hammer, *c.* 1905. Brought up at Mucomir, A.A. Cameron was to become internationally famous. On his retirement he held fifteen world records as a heavyweight athlete.

A.A. Cameron tossing the caber, 1905. This photograph was taken in New Zealand. Tossing the caber may have its origins in lifting the coupled roof beams of a Highland cottage into place.

Shinty game, Glencoe, 1920s. Shinty has been played in the Highlands since the arrival of the Gaels from Ireland in the sixth century. The three Lochaber clubs registered when the Camanachd Association was formed in 1897 were Glencoe, Spean Bridge and Fort William.

Brae Lochaber shinty team, 1926. The photograph was taken at the Cup Final in Glasgow, where Brae Lochaber lost to Kyles of Bute on a replay. Those present are, left to right, back row: John MacFadyen (ref), Archie MacGregor, Archie Cameron, Donnie Boyle, Willie Boyle, Angie MacIntosh, Sandy MacIntosh, James MacDonald (blacksmith, Bunroy). Front row: -?-, Donald Elliot, Sandy MacGregor, Angie MacDonald, Donald Rankin, Tommy Cameron, Jimmy MacGregor. Shinty today is going through a revival; Fort William won the Camanachd cup in 1992.

Curling in Glen Nevis, 1890s. The competition is between Lochaber and Spean Bridge, and there is a great turnout for the game. The rink was maintained until the late 1950s.

'A disputed point', Ardgour, early twentieth century. This smaller-scale game is on the crofters' common grazing at Ardgour where a rink was made each year. Winters must have been much colder in those days.

THE COUNTRY

*Kate MacKinnon on the beach at Morar, 1930s. The cow
is clearly a very good-natured beast and does not need to
be tethered for milking.*

After the emigrations of the nineteenth century, the population in some areas of the countryside, such as Morvern, had fallen by as much as two-thirds. Those who stayed continued on their crofts. A croft originally was a smallholding which could not support a family without income from another source. Crofters turned to fishing, or found employment on local estates. On poorer areas of land, their life even in this century was very harsh.

There are, however, areas such as Arisaig and Spean Bridge that have viable arable ground and where farming on a larger scale is possible. The evolution of Mallaig as a fishing port is another example of a more progressive economy.

Landowners fell roughly into two categories. There were Highland families who had kept their land through the centuries, the outstanding example of this being the Camerons of Lochiel. There were also landowners, often wealthy industrialists from the south, who had bought land in the Highlands for its sporting amenity. These families built large mansions and poured money into their estates, expecting and receiving little material return.

The photographs in this section are in geographical sequence, but the same themes recur.

The children from Strathlochyside School, 1920. This school group looks a very happy one.

ARDGOUR, MORVERN & ARDNAMURCHAN

Corran Narrows looking north, 1920. The lighthouse was built in 1858 by David Stevenson, one of over forty lighthouses built by the three Stevenson brothers. It marks the southerly entrance to the Caledonian canal.

Corran Ferry, early 1900s. The steamer's wake is about to cause havoc. When the Macleans drove the MacMasters out of Ardgour in about 1410, the ferryman made a major error of judgement. He betrayed his MacMaster chief to the Maclean who then killed him for disloyalty.

MacBrayne's SS *Mountaineer* at Ardgour pier, 1920s. The steamer is on her daily run from Fort William to Oban. A fondly remembered part of Lochaber's past, she used to have a permanent list.

Opening of Ardgour War Memorial, 1920. Since Culloden, the Highlands had been a vital recruiting ground for the British Army. Highland villages were devastated by the losses of the First World War; Ardgour lost sixteen men from a thinly populated parish.

Stalking party, 1920s. Lt. Col. Alexander
Maclean of Ardgour leads a party up a gully into
a stag. The lady's bold tweed is good
camouflage, as is the kilt.

Maclean of Ardgour on the hill, 1920s. The stalker is on one of the high tops of Ardgour with his West
Highland terrier (right), resting his telescope on his stick to steady it.

Maclean of Ardgour fishing in Glen Scaddle, 1920s. Among the best fishermen in Ardgour were the minister, the Rev. Alexander Maclean, and the village constable, Sandy MacDougall. This limited the poaching potential.

Building the dam at Glengalmadale, Kingairloch, *c.* 1910. This dam was built by Kingairloch Estate to create a large freshwater loch and improve the fishing. Salmon and trout fishing could, at the time, be let for a premium, and the estate hoped to boost its income.

Drawing of the Floating Church being towed into Ardnastang Bay, Strontian. After the disruption of 1843 in the Church of Scotland, the landowner at Strontian refused to give land to the breakaway congregation of the Free Church. An enclosed flat-bottomed barge was therefore commissioned on the Clyde. The barge served as a church holding 400 people for about thirty years, until she broke her moorings and grounded in the bay. A gauge of the popularity of the preacher was how low the boat sank in the water during a service.

Turf House, Ardnastang, Strontian, *c.* 1900. The old lady is Florrie Hamish. The house is made of turf built up over a framework of birch poles. This photograph is most unusual since by this era most houses would have been built of stone. Thomas Pennant, an eighteenth-century traveller, wrote that 'in this moist climate the cottages have a perpetual . . . verdure'.

Engine house at the lead mines, Strontian, 1901. The lead mines were opened in 1722 by Sir Alexander Murray of Stanhope, who had recently bought Ardnamurchan Estate from the Campbells. The mines were to help drive Murray into liquidation. The influx of miners at this time meant that Strontian was a 'scene of anarchy'. The mineral strontianite, from which strontium is derived, was first identified here in 1793 by Dr Thomas Hope. The mines have been in operation intermittently until this century, and recently byrites was extracted for use in the North Sea.

Looking north up Anaheilt, Strontian, *c.* 1900. The black house in the centre is where Rockfield now is, with (left to right) Riverview, Oakfield and Crossfield behind. Donald Cameron, the haymaker on the left, was an excellent cobbler.

Mending nets behind Strontian Post Office, *c.* 1900. Loch Sunart was at one time rich in herring; these nets were probably for cod and mackerel.

Puffer in Strontian Bay, *c.* 1900. Puffers were run aground deliberately at low tide in order to unload. The Strontian river used to run closer in to the shore.

Unloading coal at the Coal Reighe, Strontian. Coal for the community would come off the puffer to be weighed and distributed on the shore.

Achranich House, Lochaline, 1870. Built in 1866 by Octavius Smith, a distiller from London, this house was demolished by his son Valentine eighteen years later to be replaced by the present Ardtornish House. The architect for the new, and possibly the old, house was the Dr Alexander Ross who built St Andrew's church in Fort William.

Maiden voyage of steam yacht *Dobhran*, 1875. This beautiful 320 ton vessel was built at Port Glasgow for Valentine Smith. She was used by the Smiths to journey to Ardtornish Estate, and for sporting and cruising excursions.

Salen Bay, *c*. 1900. The house on the right, Duncraig, was built as a Temperance Hotel. The Salen Hotel was built next to it, no doubt with some opposition from the owners of Duncraig.

Moss, Acharacle, *c*. 1900. Acharacle, 'Torquil's Ford', was named after a twelfth-century Norseman who was pursued and killed at the ford. His pursuers were led by Somerled, who expelled the Norsemen from the west coast and established the Lordship of the Isles.

Salen Hotel, 1930s. It took until the 1990s for the sharp turn down past the hotel to be improved.

Tug of war, Salen Sports, 1931. The steward, centre, is Colonel Ronald Campbell of Inverawe, who organised the sports. Several of the five Maclean of Ardgour sisters are pulling, enthusiastically if erratically, in the left-hand team. The sports were held where the village hall is now, and were

Old Shielbridge House. This was an inn before the MacBrayne family, of steamer fame, bought and extended it in the 1890s. In 1897 Ardnamurchan Estate was bought by Charles Dunnell Rudd, a partner of Cecil Rhodes. Rudd had just finished renovating the house as his main residence when it burnt down in 1900.

Shielbridge House, demolished in 1950. Rudd built this lovely house after 1900, before building Glenborrodale House. The right-hand wing incorporates part of the previous house. The garden was subsequently laid out by Lady Clark, mother of Sir Kenneth Clark.

Dorlin House, Acharacle, 1935. The original 'Queen Anne' house on the right was given its Victorian addition after 1855, when Loch Shiel Estate was bought from MacDonald of Glenaladale. The house was blown up by the Territorial Army in 1963.

Day's catch from the Shiel, 1935. The fishermen are standing on the lawn of Dorlin House, with Castle Tioram, former stronghold of Clan Ranald, behind them.

SS *Clanranald II* on Loch Shiel, 1930s. The steamer plied from Acharacle to the railhead at Glenfinnan for thirty years. In the days of regular ferry traffic, communications on the west coast were often easier than they are today.

SS *Clanranald II* leaving Loch Shiel, 1930s. The funnel has been lowered and there is a crowd on the Telford bridge over the Shiel. The rings by which she was hauled down can still be seen.

Blackhouse at Strath, Ardtoe, *c.* 1910. The crofthouse is in a well-sheltered spot. Cattle had in the past been in-wintered in the black houses but this is a trim dwelling-house with substantial glazed windows.

Haystacks at Strath. The tiny hayfield, belonging to the crofthouse above, shows the difficulties of cultivation in the area. The croft was worked by two sisters, the larger of whom, Mairi Mhor, did most of the outside work and smoked a clay pipe.

Poruairk, Ardnamurchan, 1920s. In the 1850s the owner of Ardnamurchan Estate, Sir James Milles Riddell, had turned the farmers of Swordle off their lands to create sheep runs. The dispossessed were given land for a settlement at Portuairk by the people of Achosnich. From farming, the people of Swordle turned to crofting and fishing.

Gathering seaweed, Sanna, Ardnamurchan. Many crofting communities had been established early in the nineteenth century to collect and burn kelp for the landowners. After the end of the Napoleonic Wars, trade in kelp ash, an industrial alkali, collapsed; this was to be a major cause of emigration.

Archie MacEachern, Kinsadel, Arisaig, carrying seaweed, c. 1910. Seaweed was used to fertilise the fields. It was perhaps more common to see a woman carrying a creel than a man.

Kilchoan pier, 1920s. Hay is being painstakingly transported. A good pier was built at Mingary in 1898, but there was not enough traffic to justify a regular steamer service to this isolated corner of Lochaber until after 1945.

Ardnamurchan Lighthouse, c. 1900. Built in 1849 on the most westerly point of mainland Britain, it was designed by Alan Stevenson, the eldest of the three Stevenson brothers. R.L. Stevenson was his nephew; Long John Silver was said to be based on a character in Arisaig.

MOIDART & MORAR

Sandy MacPherson, postman, at Lochailort, *c.* 1920. The post arrived at Lochailort by rail and was carried to Glenuig in panniers.

Road to Glenuig, 1930s. It was not until 1966 that Telford's road to Kinlochmoidart was linked through Glenuig to Lochailort.

Falls of Morar, *c.* 1900. The hydro-electric scheme, completed in 1947, altered the falls. After Culloden, Government soldiers from the brig *Furnace* portaged their boats past these falls to reach Loch Morar. The soldiers were searching for the Jacobite fugitives, Simon Fraser, 11th Lord Lovat, and Bishop Hugh Macdonald, who were on Eilean Ban, an island in the loch. The fugitives had thought that they were safe from pursuit, as they had taken all the boats on the loch with them. Lord Lovat, elderly and infirm, was captured and subsequently beheaded for his role in the Rising.

Alice, Lady Lovat afloat near Tarbert, 1906. The rower is Vera Caldwell, later Mrs Basil Shaw-Stewart. The Lovats had bought North Morar from MacDonell of Glengarry in 1768; they took a great interest in the people on the estate, and there was little emigration. In contrast, many were to emigrate from MacDonell of Glengarry's remaining lands.

The *Stag* on Loch Morar, early 1900s. This elegant steam launch plied from the west end of Loch Morar up to Meoble.

Loch Morar, 1903. Morar Lodge has recently been extended by its tenants, the Caldwell family. The hill behind is newly planted. The design of the rowing boat's stern shows its age.

Interior of Morar Lodge, 1903. William Caldwell was a Cambridge don; the family divided their time between Cambridge and Morar.

Herbert Caldwell's caravan, Morar, 1903. A brother of the Morar Lodge family, Herbert toured Scotland in this horse-drawn caravan. He subsequently built Swordland Lodge on Loch Morar.

Above Morar beach, 1914. The Daimler driven here by William Caldwell had belonged to the German Ambassador, and had been confiscated from him at the outbreak of war.

Haymaking near the church, Loch Morar, early 1900s. The hay was dried initially in stooks and then the hay rick built. The figure on the right is probably a Caldwell.

Harvesting the oats, Traigh, Arisaig, 1880s. The crop is being cut and put into stooks by the MacAlpine family, tenant farmers of Arisaig Estate. Oats provided a staple food, and its straw made good cattle feed.

'Long' Angus MacDonald with a stalking pony, Arisaig Estate 1882. The pony lived to be forty, and is clearly here near the end of his working life. A modern picture would show little change; the deer saddle and indeed the clothes would look very similar.

Fishing on Loch Morar, 1894. Two Irishmen, Sir Ralph Payne Galway, on the right, and his brother, rented the fishing on the loch from Arisaig Estate. They are planning to fish in some style.

Looking out from Swordland on to Loch Morar, 1929. The haphazard style of fence in front of the black house was, in the past, a familiar sight.

Black house, Kingory, Morar, *c.* 1910. There is a washtub by the door and a plough on the left of the picture. The house's rounded corners indicate its age. The thatch was made by layering turf on the roof and tucking bundles of straw under each turf.

Cutting peat, Bourblach, Morar, *c.* 1910. The work involved several families, and took place in the late spring. The men are cutting and lifting the peats, the women and children are spreading them on the ground to dry. After about two weeks the peats will be dry enough to be propped up in groups of three for further drying. A month or so later, the peats will be carried back to the crofts and stacked.

Angus MacLellan, cutting peats in his most photogenic manner. Angus is on the right in the photograph above.

Clipping at Bracara, 1930s. Left to right: John Mackay, Katie-Mary Gillies, -?-, Ewen Gillies, Sandy-Ewen Gillies, Angus MacVarish, Neil MacDougall, Donald MacDonell. As ever, crofters are pooling their labour.

Alex MacDonald building path, early 1950s. Working alone, Alex built the path from Mallaigvaig to the family croft at Mallaigmore. Tragically, he drowned close to the shore not many years later.

Flora MacKinnon, Mallaig, 1920. Flora spoke
no English, only Gaelic.

Churning butter, Morar, 1930s. If the boy were
a little taller, his work would be a bit easier.

Iain MacKinnon, baiting his lines with mussels, Rhu, 1920. Rhu had been the pier for the Arisaig area until the new Mallaig pier was built.

Iain MacKinnon and his daughter Kate beaching their boat, Rhu. This peninsula west of Arisaig used to support a thriving crofting community.

Launching of the last boat to be built at Back of Keppoch, 1890s. The boatbuilder, Angus Campbell, is standing on the boat and the owner, Thomas Fraser of Keppoch Farm, a tall bearded man, is standing below him. Thomas was a joiner and contractor, and the boat was to provide transport to his building commissions along the west coast.

The MacAlasdairs in their 'ghiellis' at The Gurafen, Arisaig, c. 1910. Tinkers were originally the rural craftsmen; by this century they worked tin and made baskets, and picked up casual labouring jobs. They have their own independent culture.

M A L L A I G

Mallaig Bay, 1890s. After the potato famine of 1846, the 12th Lord Lovat built a pier to encourage the local community's herring fishing. The Lovats later built the salt store in the centre of the picture; the pier is just visible.

Mallaig, 1901. For the West Highland Railway to make a profit, it had to service the herring industry. In 1901 the railway was completed to Mallaig, and with the railway came the funding to build the steamer pier.

Steam drifters leaving Mallaig, 1930s. These boats often had East Coast owners, and had come through the Caledonian Canal. The kippering sheds are visible on the right of the picture.

Pier at Mallaig, 1930s. The fleet is in; the herring are being hauled out of the hold in a basket suspended on a pulley, and tipped into boxes.

Smoking fish at D.A. MacRae, Mallaig, 1950s. The shed was opposite the harbour buildings. For ten years from the mid-1960s Mallaig was the biggest herring port in Europe. In 1966 100 people in the town were involved in kippering; today there is only one traditional smokehouse left.

Joe Wiseman selling meat from Grigor the Butcher's van, Mallaig, 1930s. This is not a sight for a present-day European Community regulator.

Naming ceremony of the EMM *Gordon Cubbin*, Mallaig, 1958. A lifeboat service was established in Mallaig in 1948. The fishing fleet is in for the ceremony; the launching champagne is wrapped in a flag on the prow. The lifeboatmen are, left to right, Dod Christie, 2nd Mechanic George Lawrie, Dan Macgillivray, Coxwain Bruce Watt, Bowman John Douglas, 2nd Coxwain Charlie Henderson, Mechanic David MacMinn, Ewen Campbell. This lifeboat, commissioned until 1982, saved fifty-two lives.

SPEAN BRIDGE

High Bridge over the River Spean, before the west arch on the left broke in 1913. The scale of this bridge, rising 100 ft above the Spean, is impressive today. It was built in 1736 by General Wade, and it saw the first skirmish of the 1745 Rising. Eleven MacDonells and a piper, flitting about in the woods by the bridge, convinced eighty men of the Hanoverian Scots Royals that they were a large body of men, and the troops fled back towards Fort Augustus.

Disused inn at Highbridge, 1930s. The boy on the right is Iain Cameron, today a local contractor; he is holding a pet owl. The inn would have been a Kingshouse, a resthouse established by Wade for every 10 miles of road. The MacDonells were said to have mustered behind the inn before their successful ruse; it is feasible that they also did some of their mustering inside the inn.

Spean Bridge looking west towards the hotel, 1887. The day's work is done, and the dogs are tired enough to lie still for the photograph. Another Telford bridge, this one is still in use, having been widened in 1932.

Coming of age of Donald Walter Cameron of Lochiel, ygr, Achnacarry Castle, 1897. 'Thirty merklands of Lochiel' were confirmed on the Camerons in 1492, and the Camerons were to become the dominant clan in Lochaber. Tenants and employees are gathered in front of Achnacarry. This house was completed in 1837 replacing the one burnt in 1746.

Cameron of Lochiel family and friends, 1897. Donald Cameron, 24th Chief of Lochiel, centre, was MP for Inverness-shire and a much respected leader of the community. His wife, Lady Margaret, sits to his left. Donald Walter is on the far left, and his brothers Archibald, Ewen and Allan on their father's right.

Staff at Spean Lodge, 1887. The Davy family of Spean Lodge built St Andrew's church and Choir School in Fort William. The groom on the left is wearing a fine pair of gaiters.

Spean Lodge, 1930s. The girl is Jean Davy, later Mrs Carey Norrish. Being in service was common for country girls; many would travel south for work, and send money home to the croft. The work was hard, but it could be a time of companionship and fun.

The MacFarlane family outside their store, Spean Bridge, 1905. The present owners are the fifth and sixth generations to run the store.

Opening of Spean Bridge Golf Course, 1890s. The course was on Blarour, and was replaced by the present Spean Bridge Golf Course after the Second World War.

Boys at Kilmonivaig School, Spean Bridge, *c.* 1900. Most would wear boots to school in winter, but go barefoot in summer.

Girls at Kilmonivaig School, *c.* 1900. The school at this time would take pupils up to the age of fourteen and beyond. The level of education from these Highland village schools was outstandingly high.

The Cranachan Macdonalds, Glen Roy, and friends, early 1890s. This group of Macdonalds were from the Keppoch branch of the clan. Standing, left to right: A. William Macdonald, Blarour, later to command a Regiment of the Lovat Scouts in the First World War, and son of D.P. Macdonald, Glen Nevis Distillery; Colin Macdonald, an athlete who won admiration at the first London Highland Games in Holland Park in 1849, and whom Queen Victoria called 'my Highland stag', cousin to William; Donald Macdonald, who inherited Cranachan Farm, called 'the doctor', another cousin; Donald Macdonald, brother to Colin; Jack Macdonald, Blarour, elder brother of William, who emigrated to South Africa. Seated: Canon MacDougall, former priest at Roy Bridge; Alasdair Macdonald, brother of Colin and Donald; Father Donald MacKintosh, later Archbishop MacKintosh of Chersona, Glasgow.

The Kennedy family going to Mass, 1923. It was a 9 mile journey down Glen Roy to the old church at Bunroy. Mary on the left became Mrs Angus MacKintosh, and Ann in the middle Mrs John MacDonell. The track shows the wear of the cart wheels on the outside and the horses' hooves in the middle.

Setting out to stalk, Braeroy, early 1900s. The stalker is John Kennedy, with an English lady guest. The head stalker behind is John's father, Kenneth Kennedy. Kenneth built a school and boarded a teacher for the children of Glenturret, Annat and Braeroy.

Church at Cille Choirill, Roy Bridge, before restoration in 1932. An Irish bishop, Cairell, had established a cell here during the seventh century. This was one of the seven chapels said to have been built in the fifteenth century by Allan nan Creach, 12th of Lochiel, in penance for his violent life. In the graveyard of this chapel at the heart of Brae Lochaber lies the seventeenth-century bard Iain 'Lom' MacDonald, John Cameron 'Corriechoille' the great nineteenth-century drover, and 'Long John' Macdonald of the Distillery. The chapel was restored by subscription from descendants of Lochaber migrants based mainly in Nova Scotia.

Ploughing competition at Spean Bridge, 1930s.

Duncan Kennedy, blacksmith, at Spean Bridge
Smiddy, 1930s.

Spean Bridge, Roy Bridge and Invergloy WRIs' outing to Glenfinnan, 1939. The memorial had just been taken over by the National Trust. Standing, left to right: Mrs D. Cameron, Mrs Ryan, Mrs Bisset, Mrs Mary Campbell, 'Chattie' Macdonald, -?-, -?-, Mrs Mary MacLachlan, Maggie (Sam?), Miss Allan, Violet Buchanan, Georgie Millen, Mrs MacDonald, Mrs Strang, Mrs Clark, Kate MacKillop, Jessie MacCorquodale. Kneeling: 'Marac' MacFarlane, -?-, -?-, -?-, 'Teenie' MacDonald, -?-, Kate Boyle, Annie MacDonald, teacher at Roy Bridge, Margaret MacDonell, -?-. Seated: Mrs MacIntosh, 'Posy' MacFarlane, Agatha MacPhail, Ada Kirk, Mrs Jeannie Martin, Chrissie MacFadyen, Jean Strang, Nan Clark, Margaret Strang, Edna MacDonald, Mary Martin. Glenfinnan has a very high rainfall even by Lochaber standards, so the outing looks to have been a great success.

Unveiling ceremony at Commando Memorial, Spean Bridge, September 1952. This superb sculpture by Scott Sutherland ARSA commemorates those Commandos who fell in the Second World War. In 1942 the Commando Basic Training Centre had been established at Achnacarry, and 25,000 Commandos were to undergo its rigorous and dangerous training programme. To the right of the Queen Mother is the Rev. John Armstrong, Chaplain to the Commando Association, Brigadier Lord Lovat DSO, MC, who led the Commandos on the Normandy beaches on D-Day, and William Gilmour Smith, President of the Scottish Commando Memorial Association.

BALLACHULISH

North Ballachulish church, demolished in the 1920s. The main body of the church, to the rear, is a Parliamentary church built to Telford's design in 1829. This church was one of the forty-three built by the Parliamentary Commissioners in the Highlands. The parish created by the commissioners included Ardgour, where an identical church was built. Originally there were two entrance doors where the two outside windows are now. The window to the right of the picture is included in the present church at North Ballachulish.

Piece-time, Mamore, 1890s. The hauliers are the Cameron family, whose descendants owned Cameron's garage and buses at Onich.

Old road at Mamore, 1930s. This road follows the line set out by Major William Caulfeild, Wade's successor, when he built the road from Glencoe over the Devil's Staircase to Kinlochleven. The road was bypassed only thirty years after its completion, when the less ambitious route to Ballachulish was built.

An early coach trip, Ballachulish, 1890s.

First car crossing at Ballachulish, 1906.

Embarking on the Ballachulish ferry, *c.* 1910.

Crossing at Ballachulish: a very solemn business.

Battleship in Ballachulish Bay, pre-1914. Before the First World War the anchorage at Ballachulish Bay was said to be second in the world only to Sydney Harbour. The sheltered bay had a clay base overlaid with sand. On a windy Sunday the beach at Ballachulish would be white with the sailors' caps as they were blown off during on-board church services.

Ballachulish Bridge from the south before completion in 1975. Lochaber's road link with Glasgow was finally complete.

INDUSTRY

Bog slide on the conduit, Kinlochleven, 1908. Working in an area of such high rainfall as Lochaber can be very disheartening.

There was little industrial investment in Lochaber until this century. An exception to this were the slate quarries at Ballachulish, where a new purchaser in the 1860s expanded the existing workforce and built new housing in the village.

The first great outside investment was in 1904, when the British Aluminium Company set up the aluminium smelter at Kinlochleven. Aluminium smelting requires a lot of power, and the technology of the time meant that the smelter had to be sited near the source of the power. The entire village of Kinlochleven was built where a farm had stood before. Following the First World War a second aluminium smelter was established at Fort William, and the village of Inverlochy built. In 1962 Wiggins Teape began to build the pulp mill and paper plant at Corpach. It was intended that the mill should process the Highlands' softwood forests, planted by the Forestry Commission after 1919. The village of Caol expanded, the houses on The Plantation were built and the population of Fort William grew by 20 per cent in five years. It was these waves of investment that have caused Lochaber to change so rapidly in the last 100 years.

Looking east from Lochaber High School, 1960s. The Ben Nevis Distillery on the left and the British Aluminium Company's works on the far right are dwarfed by the scale of Ben Nevis.

BALLACHULISH

Quarry at Ballachulish, *c*. 1900. Slate has been quarried here from 1693; it is strong and of high quality. The Stewarts of Ballachulish, who ran the quarry from its inception, went into receivership in 1862 after a period of expansion. The new proprietor provided fresh investment, and by 1875 there were 587 men employed. After the First World War the Haldane family of Onich helped finance the re-opening of the quarry. It closed in 1955.

Setting the fuse in the quarry face. The blast
hole is packed with gunpowder before being
sealed with clay. The Ballachulish quarriers
were said to be the best at blasting in Scotland.

Steam engine at the quarry. This enabled
wagons on the third and highest level to be
lowered by fly wheel to the second level. The
wagons were horse-drawn; slate blocks had
finally been carried on the back in creels.

Piles of dressed slates being assembled. The quarriers worked in groups of six: two on the rock face, two on the quarry floor and two at the sheds. Each crew would have its own waggon marked for delivery to its shed for dressing.

A closer view of the shed above. The slate has been blocked out from the quarry rubble, and the man on the right is splitting it to the correct thickness. His companion is shaping the slate to a standard size.

East Harbour, Ballachulish. Slates were exported by sea. The sandy seabed at Ballachulish enabled ships to tie up safely inshore. The harbour was built of quarry rubble: 1 ton of slate created 7 tons of waste. The wagon rails lead directly to the pier edge.

Loading slates on to the boat, a closer view of above. The slates were loaded by hand in a chain or 'rank' of men. The miners are wearing their own particular brand of moleskin trousers. It was a matter of pride for the miners' wives as to how white their husbands' trousers were.

KINLOCHLEVEN

SS *Mountaineer's* trial voyage to Kinlochleven, 1907. Access to the ambitious smelter scheme had to be entirely by water. The harbour is still under construction; the bags on the pier are cement.

McAlpine's steam engine, 1908. The contracting company run by Robert McAlpine, 'Concrete Bob', had completed the Mallaig railway line in 1901, a scheme which had seen the greatest amount of mass concrete construction in the world. These construction techniques were now to be applied to the Kinlochleven scheme.

Construction of Blackwater dam, 1908. This 86 ft high dam was at the time the largest in Europe, with a catchment area of 60 square miles. Water ran 5 miles from here down to the smelter.

On top of the valve tower. There were up to 3,000 men involved in the construction works. Kinlochleven was so rough that when the weekly postman walked in he had two policemen to escort him. The navvies' tents are just visible beyond the dam.

Electric wagon hauling cement, Kinlochleven, 1908. This line ran from the smelter to the wharf. The overall impression of the site is summarised in the word 'mud'.

Garbhein Road under construction, Kinlochleven. The electric railway line is in the foreground; many of the houses are already occupied.

Factory girls, Kinlochleven, First World War. These girls were pioneers, taking on work usually done by men. They worked in the furnace room and, in time, the carbon factory. They lived in specially built hostels, and some were to stay on after the war.

German prisoners of war, First World War, Kinlochleven. Over 1,200 prisoners were sent to Kinlochleven. A legacy of their stay was 'the German road', the road that they helped to build along the south side of Loch Leven to Glencoe and Ballachulish.

FORT WILLIAM

Site being cleared for the British Aluminium Company works, Fort William, 1924. To provide hydro-power, a dam was built at Loch Treig. The water supply was increased in 1931 by damming Loch Laggan, with a water pipe link to Loch Treig. Finally in 1944 the flood waters of the Spey were drawn into Loch Laggan. The British Aluminium Company, which became British Alcan Highland Smelters Ltd in 1985, is the major landowner in Lochaber.

Cutting the tunnel for the British Aluminium Company. This 15 mile tunnel, over 15 ft in diameter, took water from Loch Treig through the shoulder of Ben Nevis to the top of the five water pipes above the plant.

The Power House under construction, 1928. The long shed that holds the power plant is half-finished, and the massive pipes have yet to be bolted into place. The engineering of this plant was outstanding.

Furnace room, 1930. The furnace room was demolished in 1981, as part of the £40m modernisation of the smelter and the merger with Alcan UK.

Puggy line, late 1920s. The 2 mile line led from the British Aluminium Company pier to the carbon factory. The rails were lifted in 1971, and the familiar bridge over the A82 dismantled in 1978. Inverlochy village, behind, is still under construction.

Engine for the puggy line, 1950s. The 3 ft gauge steam engine is shunting bauxite from the pier; the driver is Malcolm James 'Sauchie' Mackay, and the rope-runner or brakeman is Kenny Cameron.

Diesel engine of the narrow-gauge railway, 1950s. The 3 ft gauge railway ran 23 miles up to Loch Treig, climbing 850 ft. It was built to carry men and materials up to Loch Treig for the construction phase of the dam and water tunnel, but was to be in use, albeit somewhat shakily, for fifty years.

A 2 ft gauge steam engine. Balfour Beatty used three steam engines for the building of the 2¾ mile water pipe linking Loch Laggan with Loch Treig. This engine was scrapped in 1932.

Wade's Road, Inverlochy, looking west, 1929. The British Aluminium Company established the Inverlochy Village Improvement Society to provide housing for its employees. In the 1920s over three hundred houses, a shopping centre and community hall were laid out from the village green westwards. Further houses were built east of the green after 1935.

Lady Hermione Cameron of Lochiel giving a casket to the Duke of York, later George VI, Inverlochy Green, 1929. Lady Hermione is being presented by Murray Morrison, General Manager for the Highlands of the British Aluminium Company.

Inverlochy Village Hall, 1950s. This gathering of British Aluminium Company employees at 'The Braxi' includes the following: front row, left to right: Margaret Anderson, Ethel MacKinnon; second row: Beatrice Haggart, Lucy MacGregor, Jessie Flannagan, Greta Carmichael, Lilian MacIntosh, Alec MacRae; third row: Mr and Mrs John Salton, Mr and Mrs Leonard Evans; fourth row: Mr and Mrs Ainslie Nimmo, Mr and Mrs Dinty Moore, Ann Collier; fifth row: Ernie Brazier, Frank Bradley, Mrs Brazier, Mrs Bradley, Mr and Mrs John Fraser; sixth row: Mr and Mrs Michael Willis, Mr and Mrs Reid Thomas; seventh row: Mr and Mrs Ian Cassidy, Mr and Mrs Alec Fairley, Mr and Mrs Andrew Bremner, Jack Llewellyn, Mr and Mrs Fred Andrews; eighth row: Mr and Mrs Willie Cairns, Mr and Mrs Duncan Cameron; in background: Jean Haggart, Alex Bruce, Willie McMillan, Mr and Mrs Hugh Gordon.

Inverlochy Mains Farm before its conversion to the BA Club, early 1960s.

Unofficial opening of the BA Club, 1964. Left to right: A.B. Jones, Russell Johnson MP, Jennie Drummond, Gordon Drummond, -?-, Duncan Cameron, Isabel MacKay, Provost Canon George Henderson, Mr Pursloe, Iain MacKay, Mrs Jones, Mina Buchanan, Norman Goss.

Clearing of the site for the pulp and paper mill, 1963. Wiggins Teape Company invested £20m in the Fort William pulp mill and paper works, and the Government lent the company half of the cost. At one stage the mill employed 700 people. The influx of population was to have a great effect on Fort William and Lochaber. The pulp mill closed in 1980, and the paper mill, now Arjo Wiggins, makes carbonless paper, employing a much smaller workforce.

Building the water pipe over the River Lochy, 1964. The mill needed a tremendous amount of water in the pulping process. Water was taken from the British Aluminium Company's powerhouse tail race in a 3 mile pipe to the mill.

Corpach Basin, 1964. The sea lock is being enlarged and the wharf extended to accommodate the pulp mill traffic. The mill water pipe is being installed below the floor of the basin.

Caol from the air, 1964. The village of Caol grew after the Second World War, when the Council built 100 timber houses and a timber school. The bulk of the housing for the mill workers was built here, and construction works can be seen on the right of the photograph.

The Plantation from the air, 1964. This steep site on Cow Hill was a challenge for construction workers in building new housing for mill employees. Development of Fort William has always been hampered by its narrow foreshore.

The pulp mill completed, 1966. The ship at the mill pier is bringing in wood chips from Scandinavia. Two artificial 'dolphins' were constructed for ships too large to enter the Corpach basin to unload. Imported timber was used initially until the Highland softwood forests could supply enough timber. Large-scale industrial investment in Lochaber had – probably – reached its zenith in the pulp and paper mill's construction.

The first Mayday Rally in Fort William, 1974. Two hundred and seventy members of the Allied Union of Engineeering Workers are marching down the High Street. The leader of the march, on the right, is Alec Henderson, Chairman of the Lochaber Trades Council. The piper is John MacLellan and the speaker beside him is Gordon Craig from the Scottish Trades Union Congress. The second row, from the left, is Jimmy MacKay, Archie Glass and Harry Jackson. Lochaber has come full circle since the embarkations of the previous century.

ACKNOWLEDGEMENTS

Firstly I would like to thank Fiona Marwick, curator, the West Highland Museum, who has been a patient and supportive editor. The West Highland Museum's collection of photographs provides the bulk of those included in this book. I owe a special debt to Mr Jimmy Batchen, whose outstanding collection of photographs is held by the museum.

I would also like to thank Mrs Ann McDonell, Mrs Jill de Fresnes, Mrs Mary Collier and Mr George Fox, who not only lent photographs, but also helped tremendously with information. Photographs from their private collections have come from: Sir Donald Cameron of Lochiel KT, Mr Jack Shaw Stewart, Mrs Margaret Roady, Mr David MacFarlane, Mr Colin Corlett, Mrs Kate MacDonald, Mr Jimmy MacKay, Mrs Sadie Cameron, Mr Charles Ives, Mrs Chrissie Kennedy, Mr Duncan Gilfillan, Mr Kenneth MacRaild and Mr Rory MacDonald. British Alcan Highland Smelters Ltd, Arjo Wiggins, Ben Nevis Distillery, the Moorings Hotel, the Laroch Bar, the Ballachulish Hotel, North Ballachulish Church of Scotland and Kilmonivaig School have also kindly lent photographs.

With the assistance of Mr Malcolm Poole of the Mallaig Heritage Cantre photographs have been borrowed from Mr George Lawrie, Mrs Irina Stevenson, Mr Neil MacVarish and Mrs Ishbel MacDonald.

I am indebted to the Scottish Ethnological Archive (nos C14835, 18256, 18329, 18388, 18434), the Inverness Museum, the Whyte Collection, the Glencoe Museum and the Moidart Collection for photographs.

My thanks also go to all the Lochaber people, too numerous to mention, who took time to help me with queries.

Finally, I would like to thank Alex Gillespie Photography. Alex cheerfully copied an erratic flow of photographs and also lent photographs of his own.

To order any of these titles please telephone our distributor, Littlehampton Book Services on 01903 721596
For a catalogue of these and our other titles please ring Regina Schinner on 01453 731114